Streamers

BOOKS BY SANDRA McPHERSON

Streamers (1988)

Floralia (1985)

Pheasant Flower (1985)

Responsibility for Blue (1985)

Patron Happiness (1983)

Sensing (1980)

The Year of Our Birth (1978)

Radiation (1973)

Elegies for the Hot Season (1970)

Streamers

SANDRA McPHERSON

THE ECCO PRESS // NEW YORK

The Ecco Press
26 West 17th Street
New York, NY 10011
Published simultaneously in Canada by
Penguin Books Canada Ltd., Ontario
Printed in the United States of America
Designed by Chiquita Babb
FIRST EDITION

Library of Congress Cataloging-in-Publication Data

McPherson, Sandra.
Streamers/Sandra McPherson.—1st ed.
p. cm.
ISBN 0-88001-213-7. ISBN 0-88001-214-5 (pbk.)
I. Title.
PS3563.A326S7 1988   88-4253
811'.54—dc19   CIP

*Publication of this book was made possible in part
by a grant from the National Endowment for the Arts.*

The text of this book is set in Baskerville.

// CONTENTS

for Roberta Holloway
(1902–1978)
my first poetry teacher

and for Walter Pavlich

Myself: (Reading from *Pacific Intertidal Life,* to Laura Jensen)
Look at this, Laura—"Having neither heads nor tails, sea
stars change direction without turning around.
Whichever way stars go is 'forward.' "

Laura: That means if they run away from something they'll be
eaten.

Certain starfish tear or lose
an arm, a pastel wanderer,
and begin a new one.
Others cannot and learn
to hold tighter and feel with less.
                              —*Walter Pavlich,* "Sunday Aquarium"

// FLOWERING PLUM

On the sole half-day she can be alone
   she learns that there are plum-recluses,
or were, all year waiting for transparent
snowy nights in China to begin spring.
In the flowerless back of the exhibition hall
   she lies across a bench. February
in the south; people in new cloth shoes.

               Her daughter, able now to be home alone,
               leans shirtless in an open window,
                  a hermit of exhibitionism.
               Her double new ignited breasts,
               fervescent as melting ice,
               are womanly enough to bend
                  a branch, to twist a mind.

It is work to gladden your one mad girl.
   When you need to travel
she fears all scenery but herself.
You book to flow down the necks of flowers;
her turned mind balks as if *in utero*
   until you feel the blossom
force again, the doubling begin.

In moonlight which brings the woman home
her child throws a radio out the window.
   A tantrum through the thin-ply air, mist
threaded between stars. The blossom vases
shudder with the stamping of her feet.
The woman hears breakage—
   of petals, the radio caught by a tree.

Drunk, one recluse munched the blossoms
   for a midnight snack.
He made them travel down himself.
Drunk, a woman pinned some blossoms in her hair,
in the morning found damp calyxes,
   another year's seclusion.
Drunk, plums' first cold-venturing bees.

   A child hangs washed jeans to tighten
on her mother's branches,
   moss-patched, rough and twisted,
broken at their furthest, weakest reach.
On the whorl where stresses flow.
Flowering, flowing plum, winter petals:
   We are a single mother, an only child.

// LAMENT, WITH FLESH AND BLOOD

for my daughter

I do not know much about innocence
but it seems you are responsible
for this evening lake's young blue that laments
how fishermen joke and loons laugh. Sybil
of leeches, you're young but you're scary,
dangling your thin, taut, clarifying legs
at fish cleanings in the estuary.
Fog stars the knives that slip out pike eggs.
Blue's future is black. The present is rain.
The past is rain the wind blows back.
Still you sit—Audubon, catch that blue vein!—
a tiny funnel bisecting your cheek.
I want you to run to me with your kiss.
Still you brood in the lake like wild rice.

// CONCEPTION

I was seeing, as the police
came again this week, that moment
of pleasure in your student room—
carefully darkened with serious
bindings and a pulldown lamp
that left, to patrol beside our love,
only a glowing woolen peony.
Others' facsimiles of our heat that year
initiated embryos that today have pressed
our daughter against the bridge rail
and thrown her schoolbooks off to educate
commuters' tires, truckers' windshields.
Her Spanish doe's eyes now
are black with fear and hate.
                              In those days
we were translating a Spanish poem
almost gory with *rosas,* one we
finally hid from English because it had
too many *corazón*s. Into that world
we brought a child. Into our house
old pleasures have brought police.
And as one picks the softest chair
to bundle his hip revolver in,
I remember you were thinner then.

I counted your ribs.
You were starving, nearly, surviving
on corned bear-meat
which you tweezed with chopsticks.
I was fat. You sighted along my thigh
for one last moment when
there would be just two of us.

. . . And we sit now in the wooden chairs,
pinning as much hope on the officer's badge
as on a star in the blue.

// WEDDING DRESS

In the back of a shop that faced the sunset . . .

The unlifting Sound held so still it seemed fashioned
of serge, *dry* goods pleached with two depths of tides.
In the dressing room the inappropriate clothes
watched their hang in the mirror.
Before the store closes, I thought, before
the streetlights spool me home
the only survivable way, to my alley apartment
I will soon lose the thread to.

Though I approved one dress to pay the way out,
knee-length and empty of waist it is not owned.
The dress still stores the bride in her.
I unfold the pink synthetic to sniff
for anniversaries of mildew, find the oath
still caught in her old style.

Many are sewn of each design. I was just one
on such a budget who bought this look,
and must be always the poor I give it to
when I cannot give it away.

// HALLUCINATION

When I think of my bride year,
of becoming a housekeeper day by day,
of the fear you were just seeing things
in me, I remember the Revere Ware pot

with the terrible brown gurgling froth,
entrée from the night that man
you introduced into our half-furnished rooms
told us all about the *Amanita pantherina.*

You were interested
in every mystical possibility. You lined up
many poisonous mushrooms on a pine board
to shrivel across the radiator.

He said it was "a nothing experience,"
profound. For five years
he learned from it, five years without
preconceptions, nothing between himself

and the decor, the hollow
telephone ringing. Annihilation—
but like the curious
added zeroes that increase a number.

I had the sense
of air being spirited away,
of atmosphere exiled for slowing a brisk
thought, or bachelor freedom, or

for drugging a homelife terribly dull.
O his bare travelogues!—
grim for me, intoxicating for you,
in our attic apartment with waiting crib.

Spore prints, rashes as baby-talc white
as the paint crinkling off the drying-plank,
spawned unseen; all veils pulled back
for a kiss.

How I hoped nothing
                    would ever happen.
But you simmered them, skimmed off
a ciphering foam, and then
you carved and swallowed one.

Then I put candles on the radiator.
You were alive; we got back days of visions.
We celebrated *something* and the year was gone.
All the perspiring, watchful tapers fainted

into zeroes wide enough to be born through.

// ALDER, 1982

Now I will call my husband,
who entered this forest with me.
He is ahead but we both have
the white trees' strong new lamps.
He has said to be quiet,
to speak might scare a deer.
We can signal like the birds.

I prepare like a bird
the whistle that's never easy.
For birds it opens up the leaves.
As long as he whistles back
I wade in further through the sorrel.
I eat its green, and soon he doesn't
whistle back. There are purposeful
black beetles and purple elk scats
to see, and miniature red fungi
on redoubtable hair-thin stems.

I climb as one should never climb,
till I cannot see or hear him
in the dusk. And so I begin to call
with words, with symbols as green
as what consumes them.

Wrongly I fall on logs, jeans redden
with decay of alder bark,
my flashlight dead, his name
unrecognized by any tree . . .

We cannot be like the birds
so natively assured
behind their shaking, piecemeal screens.
We were not meant
for this directionless garden,
this second growth
that hides us apart.
I only know he too is calling

from his own green mountainside
at the dark that it might lift
its mask and we
be found, beneath the birds
that live continually lost,
continuously singing,
summits apart from reunion.

TWO
FLOWERS

// YELLOW SAND VERBENA

It feels as if it is going to be blown away.
And so the verbena belabors itself.
Brighter than the mossy yellow crabs
seeping in with the tide it gardens,
sticky and impressionable, it begins to collect
what's finer than gravel, coarser than dust.
Like David it picks up stones of sand, quartz rubble,
whitish, a rare orange, more populous grays
(each grain with several infinitesimal grains
of sand on *it*), until the glandular leaves
and stems grow all too heavy to fling
one pebble at Goliath.

Strange, to sit in its community at cliff-base,
trying to follow an oystercatcher's red beak
while children on the precipice lob rocks
at my head. Their accuracy brings none
of the plant's satisfaction
in its crystalline collection, gems bought only
for ballast. The stoning is mere ostentation.
I abandon the verbena for cover,
but for the umbel defense means clusters—
the deep flowers stick together
mashed or sideswiped.

This impractically lambent plant.
To be onerous is to be stable, a landowner.
Braced. Nearly stalwart.
So it will never throw plates or rocks,
so it carries them all its life,
a house of good stone stocked with china and crystal.
Nothing breaks further. The brilliant,
sweet-fragranced blossom gives the sunburned ear
beachcombing for water-music
a hemisphere of cornetti, of shawms and pommers.
And the sugarbeet-flavored root goes on living;
the villainous Philistine goes on living,
the giant who floats in next door.

// MESEMBRYANTHEMUM AND ZAUSCHNERIA

(Palo Alto Baylands and Monte Bello Open Space Preserve)

Jewels start seedy. They must crouch underfoot.
Because the rich aren't miners,
full-grown gems have an earthless style
when cleaned and heightened to a neck
or a crown. Down in the sea-winded marsh,
we kneel like lottery winners—
maybe these *are* cheap,
succulents of oozing glass,
not crystal, not silver, not ruby
but wet, seasonal facsimile.
They look like a fortune.
It is poverty, plain, to go see them
so invested in this rubbery property.

At the crossroads in the dry,
oaten, fault-ridden hills,
with most of the wildflowers driven
to seed: hummingbird trumpets,
opened like a box of ornaments.
The dust hasn't dulled them;
they lean upridge as a brush fire would.
Thatch dies and falls, thin arm
on thin leg, across their red.

We're prompted to go on forever,
but on which poor, footwashing road?
Are we cornered in passions,
ice plant abandoned
for hot-weather, hilly firechalice?
—Or delivered by them?—
The birds drink and start here,
now, to crave the south.

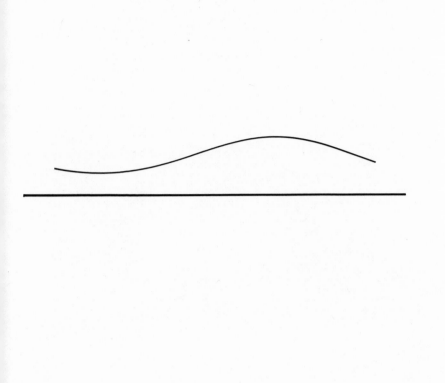

// YWCA, WILDER AVENUE, HONOLULU

The oldest rest on their beds with a book,
a head-leaned-against-the-wall look,
or head-against-the-travel-poster-on-the-wall.
The new young woman's eyes travel

down the corridor for half a dozen
smileless, contented, returned respects
which gaze out at the prospect
of the hall's long regulation against men.

Two floors of mothers and aunts of us,
airing their rooms to such ginger scents
that these debt-bare, leprous
quarters satisfy their last of wants.

They are dressed like girls again.
No coats, no heels, no shoes with sides.
They breakfast, mention chilled, gray London,
scrape off plates, and some go outside.

Here they can retire to a lawn chair
and sit enclosed by tree ferns whose buds'
orangutan-red *pulu* hair
is gatherable now to stuff the dead.

Any might be the boarder who owns
two dresses. She handwashes each,
gave up clothing to come here, dons
this morning's lagoon-bluegreen, clothespins the peach.

Is she the one I meet through her locked door?—
her weak voice answering, "I have
no schedule," mine echoing from our
shared shower, "When do you need to leave?"

Above our shared sink
a tropicopolitan pink

gecko appears. Its eyes don't track
like ours. They're big, turrety, and black.
I blink down to the basin,
look back; gone is its cream soft skin,

replaced by the peach shift's cotton
that cannot reach its launderer's long-lived, small knees.
Her humid shoulders printed with rattan,
fruited with coconut grease,

ask not to end as a cool animal
camouflaged paler in the bathroom light.
To die here is to say the whole
of each arm will show for life

under the courtyard's poinciana tree.
Not even flowers on the shirts of men
will be let in. Just blossoms growing, picked, sewn
into someone's last gift to her: a lei.

// AT THE GRAVE OF HAZEL HALL

Note: Hazel Hall (1886–1924) was author of three books of poetry.
In a wheelchair since age twelve, she lived in Portland, Oregon, with
her mother and sister. Her poems were published in such magazines as
Poetry *and* Harper's. *Until she lost her eyesight, she made her living by*
doing needlework. Her urn is housed in a mausoleum a mile from my
former home.

From the first tap on the deep stairway,
I could hear your chamber sounding nearer,
chaste studio like a shower or a swimming pool
in winter, scrubbed, swabbed, tiered with glass flower-cones
for your mourners who died long ago.

Echo of your abstemious self-descriptions,
this white-mosaicked room holds no more
important vacancy than yours. But yours was a world
in which *important* had no opposite—
a stitch pulled gravity.

Not the grand male slabs, marbled conversation of the "great
and talkative"; not those, Unvisited Vase.
Famous people may have died into the unknown
in their clubby joinery, but you
are still unknown and twin of all that mystery.

Today the messy sunlight strews
itself through bevels and brasses of your tight mausoleum.
You are drafting "Hand in Sunlight"
(you write with the other hand)

and find your thirtyish skin flushed, yellow-grooved, and pale
   blue.

The palm is gathered at the thumb.
"I am not," you conclude, "one of those too frail to sin."
Your unwalking feet are stasis; your hands, motion,
"mutually interested" in embroidering, earlier today,
the "wicked, yellow-lidded eye" of a cross-stitched peacock.

It is blinding you. To see what you still can,
you ride your chair toward the second-story window,
hold a mirror out like an insect net
for passers-by to step into.
Nainsook, linen in your lap; patricians, leaf-kickers

in your glass, with the "disputed tread"
of a too-modest woman hesitating, slowly burning through. . . .
I was thinking: Here you are,
still in your window,
in that roly-poly copper urn, a handle on each side

(for whom to hold?),
and listening for "footfalls."
I should be dancing across the tiles,
should scuff and click for you at last. Right here.
I've only brought some pussy willows to be your flower,

animal paws for the blind,
knobby twigs cut from the swan marsh.

Feel them, silvergray lanugo, cold stems clammy with memorial
   tapwater,
a bud at each twig's end the double of a deer's hoof.
Sniff the catkins—it's very faint. An aura of skunk.

"To live with Hazel
is to make one disappointed in almost everyone else,"
your sister says. She brings, at your request,
more prose than poetry. Some Frost,
Millay, and Dickinson. A lot of Katherine Mansfield,

James Stephens's *Crock of Gold* (over and over,
it is your favorite). *Jacob's Room.*
A history of philosophy that weighs your body down
so your soul can escape alone.
In these Twenties tiers and niches

many urns are books,
so many volumes with women's names,
Drusilla Salomon, a Helen Meredith.
They hoped now they were dead someone would read them.
A cinderellan library, archives of burned diaries!

But you—your turnable, unwasted pages
on death—you chose that pregnant vessel.
Chose "forcing death to approach in the rhythms of poetry,"
spurring it with your needle,
its "moving gleam like chips of ice in a heated seam,"

fusing toward this cold room of fatal fevers.

"My room?" you wrote. "Its sill
is brown, its wall is gray,
curtains of dull, sticky gold
smother hours in their fold.
The floor is not mine: always
I must waive my rights to feet."

Your feet uttered nothing. You sewed loose syllables together.
Needlework covered every surface.
"A crocus must be made so subtly as to seem afraid
of lifting colour from the ground."
But after all that keeping within lines,

you craved in language incongruity:
"a raging thread," "the glitter of sterility,"
the rip and stab among the dainty, fine
commissions from the growing families up the hill.
Liked "despair . . . brilliantly unrepressed"

and "hours of light about to thrust themselves into me
like omnivorous needles into listless cloth."
Boldly you entered the crematorium, smoky tavern
of eternal nightlife. "I am seeing so far tonight
that I am blinded by the space between me

and the inevitable. Logical smug death
takes me. The body lies unhumorous at length. The moon
bleeds gray light on the meadow
and I am weary as a sheep. I have broken with myself,
but I lie down with all the tired women,

every woman's sorrow is my own. I have given,
I have given all my hands."
                                    And on my second visit
I bring a rose. "A fibre of rain" spins down.
A bloodless electric organ eternally in sickness and in tune
plays music to another funeral. Whoever came

to yours, you never met another writer.
Your mother came to study the two urns, your father's, yours.
If she left willows, she saw within a week how catkins pushed
peroxide yellow between the gray, a moppy blossom
which, so slightly jarred, now pollinates the columbarium.

Like us she died. Like us she burned and chose to mix herself
    with you.

// THE MICROSCOPE IN WINTER

Caught in my mittens' mohair barbs—
goosedown like thrown boas of a chorus line,
evergreen needles with pitch stitches,
some wavy unshaven seeds of virgin's bower.
My eye looks down the funnel: under the light
the crooked finger of a pervert in a car;
dew in the golf-tee goblet of a lichen—
a lone crystal of glamour in a darkened theatre.
Such quiet bodies, gathered in the dusk,
thalluses and plumose fruits, silvery everything.

I bought this for a woman in crisis
so her outlook could rise
to the height of a burr
and leap the distance through a quill.
But she says, *Not yet,* feet the size
of catkin stamens. For she will study
her sleep, she says, she'll diet her curiosity,
blind to this charming mouse-food, blind
except to nightmares. She focuses on children
and we are terror. We are all too big.

Yet precisely because of your monster, dearest,
we require technology for you.

A good spider must have more eyes
than two: She needs a camera,
telescope for undomesticated space,
binoculars to hoop the faster birds.
Through these prescription lenses, face
beings who do not care you're there.
Then, to your relief, neither will you.

Boodee—dew in its eye—reflects the light,
a flashbulb in a mirror; green tastebuds
bulge all over, nappy as a rug and knotted.
Or see this red oak leaf like our mother-flesh.
Shiny. Like jerky. Or potato-chip skins
where insects chewed us for another hour of life.

It is chilly when I wrest the sweater from the tree.
Dial it in clear: There is your monster,
saying to all the larger world that scares it,
I grow kinked but not mad,
so rest on me, liverwort-haired maenad,
scientific muddy shepherdess. Look into this,
how, scintillating under battery light,
I am a greater power of moss.
My microscopic cushion shows its claws.

// EVE

Limper and meeker the cheap cottons grow thin.
Heavy with wearing things; nothing I want to be seen in.

I'd rather lean in the window
with my poppled milk-skin and say nakedness

is our drab uniform. Don't worry:
Nothing will approach, no one is looking. Only

a white dog like a flashlight across the night.
Father has allowed me to name

the clothes—as I learn to sew. But they
are boneless. They're not animals. I can't support them.

New things: Yes, I'll sit in them for a while,
a full skirt, ruffles, necklace, watch and rings,

and rub a gardener's naked back. But when he sleeps
I strip alone, open

the curtains, flatten against the window
I give oil to, pull back

with its dust tracing my sunlessness.
Or I might hold myself like rag and ammonia

to the pane I make worthwhile,
clarify. My silhouette is clearly tired,

I want to start from here and go on,
with this streaked and strapping,

purple, pale, okra-blossom bone-clothing,
the body scribbled on by a carried child

and not for young satyrs to grade. I want
the worn clothes torn

to bare the thread,
to pattern what is raw-edged.

This is my body
stitched for no one else,

with these patchworker's bloodstains—every quilt
wears its finger blood

from the needle, this
is not failure, to be harmed this way,

thimbles, bodices, all cast off. Lights off, I rest
here in a nakedness that has the power

to make our daughter
love women.

Beside the curtain torn by a catclaw
or chewed through by sun, I am more

than a glass woman, more than a fabric one.
This skin. The bible-leaves of the labia.

The fever of my forehead. Its
workmanship. Naming the quilt patterns.

Name *clothes,* Father says, be ashamed and name the clothes.

I name. Wimple, haik, yashmak. Panties, slip, bra.

// NOTE TO SAPPHO

In an age when T-shirts are our libraries,
doing laundry is a literate job.

My daughter puts a clean one on
and her seventeen-year body is an open book.

But when she takes it off, on just another
virgin night, she says Mom it's hard

to sleep against my breasts. Agreed,
but I don't curse them. Sometimes I curse

the mattress springs, get up and read
you under the lamp. Or clear-imaged lines

of my former teacher, lesbian,
you would like. Otherwise, no birds

will sing for two more hours yet.
I hand-do the indecipherable lingerie—

cups that would strain wine!
Then lie down and dream your life

linked in bumpy sleep with mine.

// ON BEING TOLD
"YOU HAVE STARS IN YOUR EYES"

(By a Man Who Denied That 95.6% of Single-Parent Households on Welfare in Our State Are Headed by Women)

The sage desert: swept in the window by a snow-broom
from the summits left white in April, with no passes.
To be registered alone, not even talking to oneself.
To want a moment's deafness to our language.
Before I'll carry luggage to the room,
to look at the crushed light in the sky;
through the opened door to see
those fires of the plain
two-eyed constellation in the mirror.

Television off, arrange to borrow a language.
Icelandic: It is a strong-toothed language with three-legged
    words
and hard-shinned sentences. Held in
Janne's dictionary: cool, full of seal-words and fish-terms,
cliff-caves and tides and hummocks of ice.
It is the size of

the infant-stones
in the narrow-running, tall-elmed Pocatello graveyard:
Their names are Chinese picture-words,
are Mexican, and Greek (with picture-pictures ovaled there).
All have become American,
all sound American now.

I step carefully, trying not to cross their borders,
while one woman digs, one woman jogs, a sprinkler whirls its
   drink,
the trees spray air with shade until it's

night: He was a salesman
of desks and files.
The man who—like a drawer against a finger—
gnashed at welfare cheats
was banqueting by now—he had to prize a woman
"Salesclerk of the Year."
He had been kind
about her, she could work the hardest.
She must be some kind of

word-witch: speaking only a strong, implacid mother tongue.
Not chat: She'd say—
                    We're always cheating
  on some guy, why not on welfare?
    Or are such ogresses imaginary?
    And can the imaginary cheat us much?
She must be some kind of skald-quean, *far-seeing witch*
to wicked women welcome always.

For she will think of the very small, their graves
the size of desk drawers. Dead before words. Lives
the shape of keepsakes, trivia, small writing tools.
I imagine, estimating by these green-glossed,
unmoving grave-lanes,
some mothers do get off relief:
for Twins Jeanette and Emma, Infant Joe and Baby Cain—
perpetual child care.

// OPENING FRED FUJII'S SHRINE

for Kay and Jim Yasutome

We found, out of all the nineteen objects
in your uncle's gritty box that wet November
anniversary of his death, two hallowed enough
for our taste: the scroll of Amida Buddha—
springy, needing to be weighted down—
no stone to him at all, thick as a cinder
of a glossy magazine in a fire
of forty-eight vows of light;

and the bell hiding under everything else,
under the little bell-shillelagh you found first.
If the Buddha wavered
like your daughter's paperdolls, the bell
when you struck it rang like my huge
and slippery breadbowl being washed—
a long sharp cry that boiled up everywhere.
Just a small *shokei* it was, a *rin.*
And a long cry coming back from everywhere.

Now each in her house alone at 4 A.M.
feels the high-strung lull
of the night shrine blacked up around us,
the objects one by one disclosed

by prowling through the boxy room
that holds us in its possession
until the god unwraps the metal idol
of ourselves, and then the paper one,
and last and last the one that's only sound.

TWO
FLOWERS

// MAUREEN MORRIS, MOTHER OF FIVE, EATS A PANSY FROM THE GARDEN OF A FANCY RESTAURANT IN ASPEN

I don't know what she'd been saying about her life.
At lunch we all shared—
pasts, minor points of minor histories—but oh
if we hadn't been chosen to live them. . . .
My detail told about a child
reeling, first time drunk, swimming
to her parents' ankles, reaching out
like a mystic gripping roots
to make it down
a steep trail to the river.

Maureen pictured us deserving better—
Carol, Ava, Lolly, the mothers—
deserving to choose what we give birth to.
And why, even, does it have to be human?
Why not that nodding purple avens in Hallam's marsh,
eyelid flower turning to feathers?
Why not a green bog orchid
more after our own kind?

And so we are waiting: It is not too late
to give birth to a flower,
never an irreconcilable seed.

Maureen heads between full tables
to a free purple face wholly open,
adopts it with a snap and eats,
passes it around our table,
does this in noon light, one bite
for each child we conceived in the dark.

// MOTH MULLEIN

Summer's mullein has returned to the field
which last fall held only spent shells, green and white
pheasant scats, furrows of dew and hunter spit.

A chivalrous opening of a door destroys
this specimen I've pained by breaking off. Can it stand
no death? Still studiously serve it

in a drink bottle refilled with carp-water
that will not settle for a week. At once
two placid yellow blossoms rust

along age-lines and drop. Each had been
a pacific, slightly downturned face
halfway up the long raceme;

white-centered fruit poised on the rungs below,
and buds, above, of melted candlewax,
short-armed and red-orange like a Bat Star.

The leaves clasp and don't wing.
Each involucre's wanded
with wet glass fenceposts unstrung. But the color of the center

grieves me, or thrills,
the purple wool costume, filaments with ready
cymbals, anthers the gold of egrets' footsoles.

A tiny green stigma is not a writer's tool.
Scoping into the center: blood-drops
on the ends of hatpins, sea-forms

like club-tipped anemone tentacles,
much cherry-dyed fringe—a parlor look.
All this

in a flower which resembles a moth
resting on a stem
at its simplest.

By the third day
four new moths arrive.
Tomorrow they will eat their woolen hearts out;

but for now they placate,
like a wall of reflections off puddles or watch crystals,
actual bodies between poppycock and substance.

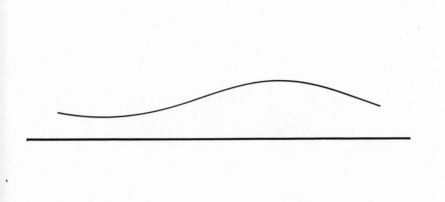

// FROM MY NOTEBOOK, CAPE COD

When I've found a patch of shells
on the usually bare beach,
or a gullet of crushed glass and rock of several colors,
turquoise and black and glittery,
then I've felt good again.
I am dependent—
without touching these things,
I haven't enough shell and bird in me
day after day to be content.
What is most spiritual? I ask a gray and healthy friend,
who answers:
In January when the rain and snow
return this shore to a fishing village,
minor miracles occur.
Another friend, young, with cancer:
Oh it's a place of desolation.
Plastic, metal, a desert where a swamp was drained,
where nothing can grow:
That is most spiritual.
In April morning light
each describes a joy
so different.
Unpossessiveness can be content that way.

But a magnate when he dies
will haunt
which of his homes?
For me most spiritual is when I walk out to the edge of town,
beside the melt-rim of the snow,
white grass rebounding in the sun,
and listen to the snakes.

// UNSPOKEN REQUEST

(Assembly of God, 1980)

Sliding across the vibrato
of a hymn, I must pick up the alto

while the other singers raise their arms
and shout with shuddering
love for the invisible

Bridegroom, honest but still to show.
We've all walked here through woodchucks,
cottontails, the low and wild

evening menaces
among the plots of cabbages
true believers keep.

We offer our needs
with "unspoken request"—a shy term to ask
for we-won't-say-what, we will think what

and moan, sleeves fallen back to our shoulders.
Homemade sleeves.

Whispering: "I have this prayer somewhere on me,
lost in my purse, stitched in a cuff.
Search me, O Lord."

// THE FEATHER

I accept its descent, a trace
of a good soul taken in the Rapture,
its barbs zipped
like the slacks of men at church.
Through quick and violent beating against air,
the vane holds, rays determine its outline, run out
to the curve and wait. There is no perimeter. The boundary
is the ends of rays. End after end.

They help us not to feel far below the higher things.
More so than kites—kites are not called upon to crawl.
But birds reach down with a hand, a lizard's inspiration

loosed, as when the heron so widely
scrapes the cobwebs from the creek bed.
Silver-gray furrows, blue and metallic tarnish on the other side.
A crimp along each row. Color of braid, of metal thread.
Color: water-surface in shade, the ripples.

At the Pacific, all loose feathers finally gather
where wind routes enter the beach grass.
They mark wind's highest tide:
an overstuffed dune.

The water pours out
of the closed heart cockle.
I have feathers, the crossed and divided, unreweavable.
They roll in the wavelets; one works like an oar on the
    seersucker kelp.

Low tide, sea lettuce dried into taut windows over stones.
I see five red mouths in a pool of crinkled whelks,
tap the barnacles so they hide their bite.
A crow plants her foot on a crab, wrings up a tuft of meat.
A single helping of elation, accessory of soaring.

When will she leave a feather of her own dismantling?
Here are enough for anyone who needs
a fraction of flight.

// THE PANTHEIST TO HIS CHILD

When I first met my birthfather he seemed to say:

Keep this picture. Here I am—
just after the war that's how we all looked,
pensive, my violin played inside out.
My head bowed down, I leaned
like someone just emerged
from a score for strings.

My philosophy's part grass, part weed.
I cultivate it and I let it grow wild,
rangy as lilacs, disorderly as chestnuts
slamming down hard
so I cannot paddle them back.

The universe needs your sympathy
even though it boos my appearance sometimes.
Religion? I went *through* Zen;
I like the tea ceremony
but have no one to spill it with.

There is one God. Whoever it is is everywhere.
In the poisonous mushroom
whose curry flesh bruises turquoise,
a blue blush, just that sudden;

54

in the hit dog, black and white, uncombed,
who sticks out his blood like a long tongue
meandering down the grade,
a death-leash;

in sex
God looks at in ecozones;
fireweed fluff lodging in a scorched slash pile
just before the snows, dodder
wrapping itself all over pickleweed in itchy marsh brine.

Do you think? Do you believe? Are some things proved to you?
That day we found one red poppy in a roadside of thousands
golden—.
Maybe it's standing up for bafflement.
Maybe it's an ancient bloodline found.
But do not believe that by being cleverly
all alone it stands for oneness.

It could be a rose fanatic, a defensive whistler,
unique in a world without tokenism.
All of these good guesses
make me a philosopher.

Ah, daughter, a kin of insight waits for you in me.

// BIG FLOWERS

Of microscopes my birthfather writes
he has bought stronger and stronger
to plumb less and less, "belly flowers"
he calls what we search for—

you must crawl to find them.
Big flowers seem easier to see.
The lilies wear more speckles.
It takes more yardage to complete

their dress. They help us to accept
our disappearing sight, the tear-film
and the blur of far and near.
Even so, Indonesian, the largest flower

is about to vanish. Not by shrinking
but by forgetting how to grow—
Rafflesia, its rainy, viny habitat sold.
This parking lot in which we kiss goodbye

must have been all big flowers once.
On the rainy, tide-deep coast, July,
my focusing daughter and I
knelt by Hooker's evening primrose,

big and busty in a suds of blackberry sprays.
I thought the Hookers
too large to be explored.
But then they confessed some small things:

how unathletic their stances are,
how they grow too floppy to be trumpets,
how they dab on far
too much perfume.

When sun rises the blossoms droop,
though they're so sulphur they'd be camouflaged
in sun. Why things grow:
A wasp wind-pollinates our hands,

a primrose caves its eight swaying
suitors and svelte pistil, buff
genders sans bulge or curve.
These are not for the scent-blind

sea-wind. Their hollow simple looseness
calls the bees, those kitbags of the senses.
Of full flowers it's not that magnitude is better;
it's that this primrose doesn't promise too much.

It carries its dead just as high
as reinforcements. Its seed capsules
big as pencil sharpeners
last into November, loaded buses

on a rainy night. And into next
century, small futuristic roe alive
with hundred-year-old curly dock and moth mullein.
Of blossoms' dimensions,

there *is* no minimum, no maximum.
Any size flower destroys
a wish of dominance; that is its duty.
The furthest flora are not gardeners' prides

but border guards at the edge of the universe,
stationed by the bay
of the nothing that lies beyond,
helping it in with a whiff of our blue air.

The spaniel-eared irises,
the gramophonic morning glories clambering
over wild cucumber . . . Before they unhitch
they hold more up

than belly flowers do. But we're not hearing
comparisons in their solar auditoriums.
Why things grow. Field guides, bouquets
do not know how to answer.

Why growing things desire even the unanswering.

(Oenothera hookeri)

SOULS
AND A FLOWER

---

the scientists can't proceed
without one of the dogs spotting them
and calling, calling a syllable
of clipped and loud appeal,
without the animal throwing itself
against the chainlink wall.
Through the vets' binoculars
it wags an indefatigable tail,
which seems to propel the others—
three acres of beagles racing,
reversing, grinding down
the runways in their cells.

They stir up drafts and eddies
in the strontium 90
they are meant to be changed by.
The doctors they're so pleased with
are returning empty-sacked
hours after the emergency call
to their raptor center—
they've been out scouting
for the hurt hawk all this time,

through wintering tomato fields,
down in creekbank brush as gold
and scratched as an old wedding ring.

I stand in the background
in the honeycombed darning-eggs
of teasel on its spiny bract-nests.
I couldn't help it; I have experimented
with the lives of those I loved.
They couldn't help
but do so too.
The pods, some haired or parchment,
bless their outgoing lineage,
however dispersed and muddied.
I am watching for something lovely,
anything in the blithe and hazardous air
the unadoptable dogs
will not be disappointed by.

The bird surgeons skirt
and disappoint the dogs.
To reach where danger ends
the people need to disappear
into the care facility next door,
between the corral of hard little goats
and the ordinary panicked
bray of the experimental mules.
And soon, as the doctors trusted,
the tirade of hopeful seeing dims
until the beagles shut entirely up
and send a hush across the lowlands
of unfound hawks.

I still listen. I don't trust.
But not a single animal whines
of all these souls in the hands of researchers

in this land of souls
waiting
for the hands of searchers.

// FRINGECUPS

Of a green so palely, recessively matched to the forest floor,
one asks if they will turn a color
for they could hardly fade more.
Around them, buttercups spread witheringly bright.

But there can be a deep pink sign of aging
on a cup's curled edge.
And when its style calves and the ovary splits,
one drop of cucumber-scented water sprinkles the fingernail.

Here I've found
the exhausted shrew, the kissy snail
in the green steam of a rainstorm.
But wildflowers do the mopping up.

Is it they who define the fringe?
Or the border made by the flooding, reddened creek
one cannot wade or swim across,
one's joy become impassable?

Not that there is anything beyond
this blurring, this infringement of full glory,
but one need, wonderer: You have friends
you are studying for degrees of bliss;

monitor this—how first I became enamored
of these fancy nothings, these teacups so small
tempests can't get in.
It was while walking out of words and into the margin

as into the missed language of a foreign film,
where all I understood was an edginess,
a century unrevisable now, a humor sometimes sexy
and ending in death

like the occasional red lips of one strap of fringecups
in the midst of all the green ones.
By the time anyone might read this
it will be very much too late

for the fringecups' unconfident bells
and yet we will want to keep on
hearing something. They looked
like sound. They led us to believe they could ring.

Where did that strength of illusion come from?
The fringecup evanesced when the weather
turned sunny. Its whole modesty now is gone.
No boasts are in its place.

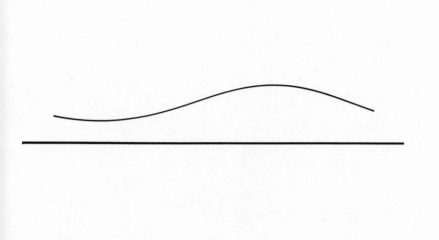

// STREAMERS

All the women who leave tell me they're happy.
But my friend, kneeling with me, is the only

one who goes on living by herself
and owns five houses,
one of them on land sloping to an "arm of the sea,"

silver and indigo, young salmon worrying,
stealing anchovies schooled up.

The sea which dangles, this August forenoon,
from the thumb of a dock
a stunning swimmer, leaning against plush

sea-fans and kicking
her warp of tentacles
slowly out across the current.

We've dropped to our elbows.

       I remember winters here,
       frost on the wharf
       so long you could mow it;
       a consumptive ship,

the Barbarossa,
pumping out basements-worth of water
all day, all dark,

water that made it
sink inside
outside buoying it light.

You could touch its rope
and draw the huge ship near.

And this *cyanea* is as big
as our daughters,
as long as my friend's old bridal veil

(I wore a scarf)
perishing under woolens in a steamer trunk
on an attic voyage.

The rest of its ensemble imports
from Spain: tiered flounces, bunched bodice,
and bolero, mostly
of a salmon-watermelon-shrimp

or peach-ginger pastel; lips
and gonads tucked into a skirt
scalloped into eight notched lappets

weighted with a crystalline rhopalium.
Such is the fashion.

    "Women have so seldom
    been an attraction to me,"
    said Sherlock Holmes in "Lion's Mane,"
    "for my brain has always governed my heart,

    "but I could not look upon
    her perfect clear-cut face,
    with all the soft freshness of downlands
    in her delicate colouring,

    "without realizing
    no young man would cross her path unscathed."

    Ah, friend,
    not only must we scathe,
    we must also know the remedies:

Ammonia, vinegar, or meat tenderizer,
papaya juice, gasoline, olive oil,
ocean water (never fresh).

Remove tentacles with a gloved hand,
apply flour, baking powder,
shaving soap.

Come to the sea with these.
Then scrape.

And yet her clear head
of flawless Orrefors . . .

Dilation, contraction.

Do you recall the day
of our equal depressions?
My husband telephoned back and forth,
listened to you then to me,
unable to synchronize our calls.

He described us to each other.
Then he went fishing.
He navigated through the Lions' Manes,

obnoxious, cursed—
one cannot touch them, tear them
off a line—

and ran his boat elsewhere,
to other animals,
seals, puffins, dogfish

nipping away at bait and catch,
skill, success, and hunger.

You and I were in some depth together,
miles apart, he said

and it helped.

Now, perhaps, we've begun the migration
(if only our third friend were here,
and our fourth . . .).

The woman in the Marine Science Center welcomes
these medusae every August warmth,
holds out her arms to show

how big she's witnessed them.
But for now our arms and knees support

not any frozenness
but our still undistraction,
a concentration on the pulse

that is not stone
and turns no one to stone
who really stays to see her.

And she leans there, greeting, in her door,
all current, streamers, tired and toxic

but striating, ruffling,
armlessly herding eggs
like transparent hotcross buns.

Our hair hangs over the dock,
her tentacles eight-hundred, nine-,
pulling us out of the rock,

relaxing, flexing.
She is unparalyzing,

no hard parts at all,
and she is all alone.

// LEDGE

Butterfly-lily
and roan puff-pea
raise a sparse meadow
in gravel.
So does a patch
of snow downslope,
solitary and dirty
like a goat.
From timberline
Jeffrey pinecones
roll into the lake.
Clothes lie on a rock.
I too
float into Lake Shirley.

The bottom atomizes
at a toe-touch,
disperses upward,
rapturizes
its green, hairy,
restless insolidity.
The lake floor
is suspense.

Human presence
shoos like a draft
its elderly
incohesion—
each fathom sneezes
to my step.

"Follow the outlet
down and never,
never go uphill."
But a hawk's back
reddens and veers off—
below. A short
shore where I drink from my hands
bridles into a cliff,
an inchworm
rears its waist
to read "omega."
And the dropping
low voice of the stream

teases me
to suspect I climb.

Until across an aeon-cut
between summits
sulfur as a Zen wardrobe,
not snow
but something freshly
fallen there—
a white crash,
a private patch
of plane,
which the rescue helicopter
at frost-dawn yesterday
frowned upon

and today newsprinted
as waffled wings,
an engine's deep
metal eyes
in a burrow,
a meteor, a marmot.
Here on this ledge
the strange
stream I must follow
splits two ways.

A water ouzel
turns its tail,
uncurious, calm, and gray—
oh but even he

must see this:
how a guide of water,
slipping and falling,
does better than a person
trying to descend
alone, keening
to belong
in the grassy,
red-ant valley
a day beneath
this ledge
from which Shirley Creek
hangs in two sashes
such as my lost

grandmother used to tie
behind me.

I crouch at the knot
in a print of odors
of Jeffrey lemon
bark, twigs
snapped cold as vanilla,
violets, pineapples,
apples: illusion,
a high
to cover the hard panic
centered
above two waterfalls
growing apart.

I like granite.
It can act like a tin basin.
But I wish I were not
alone, unsure,
and strange to the ouzel.
I feel the quartz rapids,
shallow-grained, deep-striped,
trying to twist the water
round my little finger.

Springy, it all
loosens of itself.
Goes where?
Past, past where
I lift off my shirt
              and wash.

// DEEP GRASS, MAY

Nootka roses, black-seeded mustard, white-flowered
hawthorn with small leaves—
and in between by foot
we map the grasses,

from the chewed-down blades
that whisk the pasture
to the long and polyknuckled
herbs catching at hair.

They count, singly. Sometimes add up
to a cheap haircut on an inconsistent head.
Their ascension grows into stooping.
The straight line falls in a curve.

Black-outlined oatlike purple scales
edged in silver awns
spike stems out where fish are spawning,
where flooded evaporating fields

steer carp's coined backs
around the sky. An aquarium
armored with conquests, unchivalrous.
Their love will dry for grasses.

At home I've grown a grass garden.
I've let all hinge on accident.
It grew after the uprooting:
"The forsythia was a pain in the ass,

the chrysanthemums always falling on their faces . . . "
the owner said. The cherry tree too—
he yelled "Timber"
and it fell on the birdbath;

now we have no problems with roots.
Yet there is a house—grown from roots:
Out here on the levee the loose conducting seedheads
of the rangiest green stalks

presuppose a music passing through its walls,
a house as no developer would have built it,
with crushed grain floor, the strands
of its carpentry

reaching to a depth
that changes the people we hadn't time to be
into fawns and snakes and quail.
It is all the peaces to be found there,

peace of barley, intimacy of cheat,
the snarly, silky wild carrot to bloom next month,
the heart
on the sleeve and the shirt off . . .

We'll fall as grasses fall—with no placement.
And we'll run but never truly run from it,
from our only room
a storm fills up with hail.

// WILD RADISH

"I'm not the darling here."
—Letter from a friend

The sea is seemingly fragrant today; the flowers not.
Most of their postures are crooked,
as if from too much curiosity.
Wild radish and jointed charlock fly from a gray glass,

propeller-shaped flowers white with blue veins, yellow with coils
of subsurface green like wires in an electric blanket.
The blossoms come out of a narrow green sac—
compressed down sleeping bags, the veins

sealed in with bubbles of cells like toothpaste.
Long-waisted siliques still stout,
taut as men's bikinis. Agronomist's advice—that they be burned.
But I have no field. I like an unstyled bush.

July 18. Cut off, they go on making seeds,
nine vessels of wildflowering plants—
the botanists are annoyed with half of them,
classifiers of the Fifties before weeds

had any civil rights. Hedge nettle, smartweed, sheep sorrel,
beach pea. English plantain like matted old deaf dogs.

Each plant unloved
by the authority who defines it.

Each flower scorned yet waxing sexier.
Even the grass the cucumber lassoed
is hung with sticky yellow scrolls.
What falls is beginning to make an earth—

seeds, petals, stamens, a soil.
Searocket curvings with yellow pollen tips—
as if a Persian typesetter spilled a ghazal.
The water in its topaz chalice thickened, syruped.

I'm stretched out on a sand-roughened sheet,
comparing this messy congregation to Morris Graves's
paintings of winter bouquets, haunted flowers,
in which we see nothing adorable

but favorites of a different sort,
flowerheads blacking out in a void
or stunned at their breath in the cold.
None of them is darling

but we favor an eclipse with our blurring presence
when we do not have each other
root to root in beds that nurture us.
With wiry body of bare stems, the radish surrenders.

I do not want to neaten its dropped clothes, spilled powders.

// ALPINE TWO-STEP

Taking our act
of seizing the anxious moment
on the road,
the narrow one
cut long ago
through the alps
of white trees,
we danced
with our backs
to a rockslide,
my red shawl
winding around us both
to curtain our arms
against mosquitoes,
the car having stalled
unable to breathe
as well as we
atop the talus's
slow rush
into the white roar
of the cataract.
It was that old
social dancing
of hanging on,

kissing you up under
the cheekbone's own
high altitude,
blue spruces, milky
aspen trunks, the
spiny rose
pink against
the hard-skinned backs
of moved boulders.
No one stops
to help, no one
stops to dance,
they're on their way
to the Divide
which we have known,
which we have
united
as if its two slopes
were lately partners
barely touching
above the clean, gray
avalanche
whose final stones,
arriving,

speed up the music
of the river
despite how slow
"Young and Foolish" is,
the inapplicable
beautiful ballad
we are in rhythm with.

TWO
PANICLES

// ELEGY FOR FLOATING THINGS

    An uneven basin
where presences are floating,
venturing about a plane,
the impressible surface of their bath,
a worldwidening rock tub
seismic, saturated to its core:
But, up on the tension,
determined dead things glitter
as if in new youth:
a white sea sponge, light tubes
and flares of its fermented skin,
drifts with skim-white bulbs
of giant perennial kelp;
the eddies of a by-the-wind sailor
dry to paper even as they spin;
and parakeet-green strands of surfgrass
wind from pool to pool,
some transparent person
sleeping in that hair.
A dead beach squirrel—
riding through a channel, sleeping too.
Moth with a brick-colored spot on its back.
Crab-claw. Seagreen inner chiton plates
above blue mussel coinage.

Broken, breaking bits of range.
Untied things, a mess
floating above its shelves,
a feast that will not set its table.
Cormorant feather; red sea-brush, fernlike;
separated bubbles; sperm.
Then you the collector
wedge into a seastack corridor
before a rising wave, your notebook
slipping, just for a moment buoyant,
drowning, outrushing, redisplaying,
all you hoped would be incoming,
become a terrible lesson in floating.
—Then I am in, kneedeep, waistdeep,
arms diving for it, your eyes disputing
it will sink. You cry out
that it is *there,* its ink
on the next unrolling wave-curl.
And it is in my hand,
a continental crumb,
kept whole by the hull of its binding,
all your outpourings, right words
taking rescue lightly—
for they were at last effortless,

pleased that they displaced
the pain of a slow hand.
So let them not cause panic now.
They will be taken out of your hands again
and into such good company,
ghosts scattered and wet,
to travel where lifting water carries them—
through all the linked pools.

// KINDNESS

Fuchsias in silhouette;
a "buoy that is the first note
    of the mourning dove";
        inside a motel room, one hard mirror

reflecting another mirror
into which soft dusk has marched.
    Moonlight: Rays
    of glaucous marguerites

stay open. One ten-petaled passion-
flower says it's through
    while another begins
    red night and I think

how having chosen this love
I have wanted the way there is
    no tension ever in your hands.
    These premises of your kindness

meet wind-disturbing pines
and trawlers with their arms out in a harbor
    that makes you exultant
    beyond your self-reckoning—

"mentally ill, affectionate,
just like my cat." I am arguing
      with an admired book
      upset with itself,

its love of nature quarreling with
its suspicion of the apolitical.
      Embrace weeds, it says,
      but take a stand.

I am unsure what a life
entirely of our decisions would be.
      Nothing, nobody
      would get to choose *us,*

if we didn't want, nip us,
pinch us, brush us, widen our skin.
      Ferns and a monkey flower—
      borrowing new caution, I wonder

how much we want to hear
of how graceful the earth is, thought
      after thought about its
      foliate, sturdy fabrications

and not its untender people,
its irritables and self-harmers.
 Yet, devoted to a screen of
 toasted-yellow quakinggrass,

we can choose whether
to lie like it and resemble
 a snake's rattle
 or opt to plant ourselves

over the cliff and be
instrument to the thermals,
 small sounds large
 to the insects and true.

You have elected not to threaten,
and suffering people come to you.
 I've tested the life
 where one crouches in a closet,

a voice detesting the alto
of her own pleas.
 But as this or that flower
 is kind to a pulse

and failing heart
if looked at as an equal—
    a batty little plantain
    or a poppy with orange pollen-shadows—

we are equal naturalists in love
and you are mercy throughout every day.
    If I am angry you take
    the even surface of those hands

and slowly, growingly ramble me
like a rose in a coastal garden;
    you have small temper,
    so we can notice

the wave-dash for itself,
and on the bay behind it
    fugitive jade wind-phalanxes
    for their momentary cooperation.

If I ever again see
a snappish storm against me,
    I'll know its violence
    hurries to flee loving.

It is the opposite
with your kindness. Your kindness is like
　　the privacy of the blue view
　　that shutters octopuses and wolf-eels:

It acts as though it knows them,
it works to broaden, then it covers
　　with effortless power
　　their misunderstandability.

This is the way you argue:
"Nothing in my life has prepared me
　　to be chosen by
　　the things that I love."

(Albion River mouth at the Pacific)

NOTES

"Flowering Plum": See *Bones of Jade, Soul of Ice: The Flowering Plum in Chinese Art* (Yale University Art Gallery, 1985), which accompanied the exhibit of flowering-plum art at the University Art Museum, Berkeley, between January 23 and March 24, 1985.

"At the Grave of Hazel Hall": The poem makes a collage of lines taken from Hall's three books: *Curtains, Walkers,* and *Cry of Time.* Some of the poems are reprinted in her *Selected Poems,* edited by Beth Bentley and published by Ahsahta Press, 1980.

"On Being Told . . .": The phrase *"far-seeing witch / to wicked women welcome always"* is from the Icelandic poem "Song of the Sybil."

"Opening Fred Fujii's Shrine": *Shokei* and *rin* are Japanese bells.

ACKNOWLEDGMENTS

Grateful acknowledgment is made to the following magazines and presses for permission to reprint poems which have appeared previously: *The American Poetry Review:* Conception; Moth Mullein; Eve; Streamers; Deep Grass, May; Big Flowers. *Anno Secundo:* Opening Fred Fujii's Shrine. *Antæus:* Alpine Two-Step. *Field:* Hallucination; The Microscope in Winter; From My Notebook, Cape Cod; The Danger Is,; The Pantheist to His Child. *The Georgia Review:* Lament, With Flesh and Blood. *Grand Street:* Wedding Dress; On Being Told "You Have Stars in Your Eyes" . . . ; YWCA, Wilder Avenue, Honolulu; Fringecups; Ledge; Unspoken Request; Elegy for Floating Things. *The Iowa Review* © University of Iowa: Maureen Morris, Mother of Five . . . . *The New Republic:* Note to Sappho. *Trilobite Press:* Mesembryanthemum and Zauschneria. *Verse:* Kindness. *The Yale Review:* Yellow Sand Verbena; Wild Radish. *ZYZZYVA:* Flowering Plum; Alder, 1982.

"The Feather" originally appeared in *The New Yorker*, 1985.

"At the Grave of Hazel Hall" first appeared in *TriQuarterly,* a publication of Northwestern University.

One epigraph to the book is from the last stanza of "Sunday Aquarium" by Walter Pavlich, as it appears in *Ongoing Portraits* (Barnwood Press, 1985).

My gratitude to the Trilobite Press, Trace Editions/Janus Press, and Owl Creek Press for the chapbooks *Responsibility for Blue, Floralia,* and *Pheasant Flower;* and to the National Endowment for the Arts, the Oregon Arts Commission, and the Ingram Merrill Foundation for their essential financial encouragement; and to the University of California at Davis for a 1986 Faculty Research Grant. Thank you, Diana Dulaney.